ULTIMATE BUSINESS MARKETING PLAN

(Generating Leads Made Simple): Get those customers, make him come back, make more money & stand out from the crowd.

RICHARD J. BICKFORD

TABLE OF CONTENT.

CHAPTER I

OVERVIEW

The power of 100 million leads
The only way to get money is to sell things. Everyone tries to jump to the "Make Money" portion, even if it seems simple. I tried, but it isn't effective. You need every part. Selling a product requires having clients (sometimes referred to as "Leads"), who you must then persuade to purchase it (also referred to as "Sales"). Once everything is set up, you may begin making money.

While definitions of "leads" vary, most agree that leads are the first step in gaining additional customers. It just indicates that they have the wherewithal to invest and the issue to solve.

As you are well aware if you are reading this book, leads don't appear out of nowhere. You have to obtain them. More specifically, you need to make it simpler for them to locate you so they can buy your products. The best part is that you don't have to wait to have people find you; you can do it instantly. You do this by employing advertising to generate awareness of the products you sell, which in turn results in the sale of further things. Selling more products will earn you more money.

It's hard to be poor when you have a lot of leads.

Second chances are hard to come by in the cutthroat world of business. So, loading up makes sense. Selling skills are valuable. This book shows you how to do it.

You will have access to an infinite number of potential customers thanks to this book.

CHAPTER II

STRATEGIES FOR INCREASING SALES IN

Let me be really clear and concise about what I believe to be the second most important business rule.

Selling is the most significant responsibility you have as the owner.
The most important responsibility for every founder or owner, as well as for any firm, is to sell. It's not something you can outsource, completely delegate, or perform as a side project.

The success of your business as an entrepreneur is solely dependent on how well your sales and marketing produce new money, regardless of how fantastic your product or service is.

The success of your company is unrelated to your team, your enthusiasm, your ambition, or your desire to assist others.

If your company is a well-oiled engine for generating leads and sales, bringing in hordes of new customers every day like clockwork, then owning a business can be an incredible experience.

If you don't, running a business can be erratic, untrustworthy, and very stressful. This is because your business's future, your income, your family's income, and the income and families of your employees will all depend on whatever misfortune you are dealt.

There are two options available to you: either you read this book from cover to cover and ensure that your business does not become just another depressing statistic, or you choose to ignore these facts, close your eyes, and persuade yourself that "everything will work out fine."

Strategic versus tactical marketing

A marketing strategy is a series of actions conducted to attain certain goals, and it is a long-term plan to engage with target audiences to achieve those goals. An alternative perspective is that your proficiency in marketing serves as a tool for carrying out your business plan.

Regardless of how many tactics a team employs, there is typically only one main task. For instance, a company may decide to promote its goods and services in order to concentrate on raising brand awareness.

They can accomplish this by employing tactics including product launches, marketing engagement, lucrative marketing, and sponsorship searches.

Techniques for Marketing to Boost Sales

1. Direct Marketing: Use outside marketing techniques to connect with consumers where they are. It's always a task to get your name in front of folks who aren't making calls.

When your target market is unaware of the answer or you require fast results, this marketing tactic can boost sales. However, you don't want your message to be seen by too many individuals. Research is needed to determine who will gain more from your website or contact details than from handling your information.

Outbound Marketing Strategies: Cold Calling or Cold Emailing Advertisers in Print, TV, and Radio Second, Direct Marketing

2. Inbound Marketing: Compared to external marketing, inbound marketing employs distinct tactics. Making sure that clients who are looking for the things you offer can find you will help you improve sales. By prioritizing education, you may assist individuals who are unaware they need assistance. Although nobody enjoys being marketed to, effective marketing will persuade

your clients to recommend your goods and services to them.
One must remain aware of evolving demands in sales and marketing.

Information in this marketing plan is intended to provoke individuals to evaluate your brand, look for clarification on issues, and consider making a purchase. Outbound marketing might not be for you if you're looking to close business rapidly because it takes time to advertise and get results. First, let people browse your website.

This involves a great deal of SEO and content production. But if you put in a lot of effort, you may keep driving up sales at a cheaper cost.

Strategies for Inbound Marketing

Advertise your material online with SEO

3. One-off promotion

Nobody enjoys considering themselves to be a minority. This is where customized marketing comes in handy. If your marketing isn't personalized, 72% of consumers won't even connect with it, and 80% of them are more likely to make a purchase from a company that provides them with a personalized experience. Furthermore, employing this marketing strategy does increase sales. The ROI on tailored advertising is 20:1.

This approach combines intensive research and audience segmentation with both outbound and inbound tactics to deliver messaging that is incredibly focused. It is therefore more challenging than other marketing strategies. But these processes have been made so simple that even tiny enterprises can perform them thanks to automation and other MarTech solutions.

Techniques for Tailored Advertising: Segmented Email Marketing

chatbot for computerized advertising 4.

User Content Attracting clients is especially challenging in the sales and marketing sectors, which are currently among the least trusted. Audiences actively doubt everything the firm says, as opposed to expecting expertise and education as in the past. You should thus use case studies to concentrate on what other people are saying about your brand.

User reviews, press mentions on other websites, and customer connections on your website could all be useful marketing techniques to boost sales. Instead of pushing your message on indifferent folks, highlight satisfied customers.

Public relations content marketing through the use of third-party content (Case Study)

5. Take note of the brand narrative

Your salesmen are the most precious asset in your organization and won't sell unless they give you a contract. They maintain brand awareness, adjust their messages, interact with your audience, and do much more. Thus, one of the most crucial and successful business techniques the organization may employ to boost sales is collaboration between the two groups. This can be deemed non-strategic due to its ongoing nature, rapid changes, and need for several results in order to be successful. Making sure that your leadership is in line with your primary goals and maintaining regular communication with your staff at client meetings, site design, and other events can help you make your business visible and approachable to clients.

Techniques for Telling Stories About Brands

- Web-Based Marketing Resources
- Sales Education
- Utilize These Marketing Strategies To Boost Sales

For sales to be successful, there is no "best" or "right" marketing plan. Which location is best for your firm will rely on a number of factors, including size, ownership requirements, target market, and investment requirements. Naturally, as your company develops, it's critical to assess your strategy to make sure it remains the ideal one for you. It makes sense to choose the correct course of action if your circumstances alter after selecting it, even if it takes years. But now that you have a solid grasp of both your industry and your rivals, you can select a plan of action to implement it swiftly and effectively and begin selecting the initial approach.

Determine who your target audience is.

You can't please everyone if you attempt to please everyone. Correct?

Furthermore, you won't succeed in marketing if you attempt to reach everyone. Viewers of your advertisement or website are welcome. However, neither your advertisement nor your message will be received if you do not have a precise target audience in mind.

It's crucial to identify and invest in your target audience as soon as possible because of this.

We will provide you with all the information and advice you need to finish this assignment in this book. A target audience is the particular set of people you wish to promote to. This means that your email text, quotations, and story lists should all be directed towards this particular set of people in your marketing materials.

Audience versus Target Market

Here are a few terms that need to be rapidly defined: your target market is not the same as your target audience. Your target market is the group of people you intend to sell your goods or services to.

The particular demographic within your target market that piques the attention of your target audience is your target market.

Thus, for instance, if small firms are your target market, local business owners or business consultants will be your target clients. or perhaps the three of them. Within its target market, a business may have multiple target audiences.

Here are some additional target market examples:

- assisted-living facility
- Seniors are the intended audience.

The first target market is the New England region's senior population.

Second target market: Working-age adults in the New England area with aging parents.

transferring company

Market niche: people-moving

First target group: apartment dwellers in metropolitan areas

Suburban families are the second target category.

- PPC scheme
- Small businesses are the intended audience.

First intended audience: local service industry owners

Small business marketing directors make up the second target group.

Each campaign you create will also have more focused, smaller target groups. Actually, HubSpot discovered that the majority of marketers produce content for three main audiences.

Why is having a target audience necessary? These images demonstrate how crucial it is to comprehend your target market. It offers the framework you require to create messages and content that will be memorable. PPC software suppliers catering to small business audiences differ greatly from those catering to larger enterprises in terms of branding and marketing collateral. The advertisements created by senior communities for the elderly people will differ greatly from those created for adult offspring taking care of aging parents. distinct target audiences

This enables businesses to have a broad target audience and enhances the focus of marketing campaigns and objectives. There are numerous marketing tactics that are really detailed.

For instance, if you own a landscaping business, you may target more consumers in a specific city by holding an event or giving a single discount to all of them.

However, when attempting to identify your target audiences, you should focus on those that correspond with the marketing channels you regularly utilize. Here are a couple such examples:

Email: You may have a lead-focused nurture email flow, a newsletter with advice for your entire target market, and/or trigger emails for your existing clientele.

Event: Depending on who your target market is, you could host a neighborhood-wide gathering, as the landscaping business in the previous example did. You may even throw an event for your current clientele or possible business associates.

Community: You could run a similar community that connects consumers of your product, or you could run a Slack or Discord group that matches prospective customers in relevant roles.

Advertisement: You can run Facebook ads that promote recurring business, Google ads that target prospects searching for a solution, or Instagram shopping ads that target the customers of your competitors.

social media: You could upload a how-to video for prospective customers, a thought leadership piece meant for influencers who would spread it, or audience, include writers, famous people, or subject matter experts

Guidelines for identifying your target market

To identify your target demographic, take a step back and consider branding in general, a particular marketing channel, or a particular campaign if you're unsure. By analyzing who engages with your product, brand, and marketing, you may identify your target market. This is the method.

1. Consult with your clients

Examine the people who follow you on social media. Examine the KPIs pertaining to your marketing performance. Pay attention to objections. Determine who you are not aiming for. Begin with your clientele. Your consumers are the ones who utilize your product or service, therefore it's obvious that how you position it, how you solved the problem, how you sell it, or some mix of these, worked. It is therefore a great place to start. Examine the customer experience first.

Find out their age, occupation, and place of residence. What patterns did you observe during the process? Keep a tight eye on the habits of your devoted clientele.

2. Look for trends among your past clients.

Speaking with customers is the next stage. This is the best approach to learn why customers adore your brand, people, or anything. This will assist you in deciding on your stance as well as the benefits you wish to emphasize in your interactions and copy. Finding out where customers spend their time and receiving recommendations from them is another excellent use of this time. Is it a reliable business, trade publication, or Instagram influencer's blog? You may utilize this consumer data to prioritize your marketing channels, which makes it an excellent source of data.

3. Examine your fans on social media

To find out who is most responsive to your present marketing, you may also look at your social media following. It also aids in identifying the clients who are genuinely interested in your business. Following firms on social media is most frequently done to take advantage of discounts, keep up with business news, and discover new goods and services.

It's possible that your consumers have greater access than your followers on social media. Make sure your questionnaire is brief and limited to pertinent topics if you would still like to be interviewed. If not, observe the populace and their actions.

4. Examine your rivals

There is resistance in your path. There is competition regardless of the product you sell, your target market, or your product. They are also useful to you. Examine the target audience that your rivals are aiming for. Where do advertisements show up? Facebook? Instagram or Twitter? Who are they aiming their advertisements at? Which issues are you currently facing? Create a target demographic and assess the similarities and contrasts between your own messaging, advertisements, and brands. You can sense the difference and find a better fit together. One can describe brand distinctiveness more effectively. You want to make sure that the audience your competition is targeting is actively engaging with your content in addition to the audience that your opponent is targeting. Examine his social media following to find comparable and dissimilar accounts.

5. Establish Objectives

Although it may seem strange from a procedural standpoint, the final step is crucial. You must ascertain who your non-clientele is. We now review all available data, including competition comparisons, website traffic, social network subscriptions, and customer interviews.

After that, it ascertains which blanks are most likely to remain unfilled. Are there any pet shops without reptile enclosures? Your target market does not include iguana owners.

Are you selling milkshakes with alcohol? Attracting individuals under the age of 21, regardless of their photogenic similarity, is not our objective. Are you able to just serve US clients? If yes, your intended audience does not include anyone who operates outside of these limitations. Establishing goals supports marketing initiatives as well as company strategy.

6. Developing a target audience profile

Compiling all of the data including anecdotal information about your clients, statistics about your followers, and competitive information into a target audience profile is the final step.

The following information is added: Age, gender identity, place of residence, employment, level of education, income of the household, interests, pastimes, and platform usage. The details of the profile of your target market will also apply to your brand.

Here are some examples of target audience profiles:

- new dog owner in a metropolitan area
- College senior without a strategy for their future
- A trained chef employed outside the company

Using this data, you should construct personas for team communication.

These are complex, made-up personas that stand in for certain target market consumers.

An illustration of the intended audience To further your comprehension of this concept, let's examine a few target audience examples from well-known firms.

One untamed

Assume you are a vendor of dog accessories like leashes, bowls, harnesses, and toys. Dog owners are the target market in this instance. User-generated content, such as social media advertisements, newsletters that highlight the best dogs of the week, blogs about pet care, and white papers for prospective pet owners, can help you reach your target audience. Your brand is simple, sleek, and sophisticated. Young millennials or Gen Z who are unfamiliar with dogs and other companion animals are the target market for this marketing effort, according to Airbnb

Ad is obviously directed towards adventurous dog owners.

Would dog lovers respond the same way to similar ads that featured a cheerful individual carrying a bag with a bullet point indicating that there are hosts who welcome dogs? Nope.

But Airbnb also advertises to young couples, single professionals, the elderly, and a variety of other demographics.

Target markets for Armour and Nike

While both Nike and Under Armour want to attract customers who purchase athletic and leisure gear, their target markets are very different. Nike is a high-end company whose advertisements target influential people and those in their mid- to late-fifties. Conversely, Under Armour is predominantly a male-oriented brand that caters to Gen Z consumers between the ages of 18 and 25. It is not meant for those with high incomes.

target consumer for Dunkin' and Starbucks

contrasting Dunkin' and Starbucks. College students and higher-class professionals are Starbucks' main target markets. With its in-store items, healthy cuisine, comfy couches, and free WiFi, it appeals to consumers who want to enjoy their coffee while working, conversing with someone, or having some alone time (while also conserving the environment).

Conversely, Dunkin caters to customers who are on the go and have smaller budgets due to its affordable prices and limited in-store experience (because Dunkin is the national beverage of the United States). It also affects the eastern part of the United States.

Make use of the identified target audience.

Understanding your target market in great depth is important, but it's not the last step. If you want your marketing to be more successful, you need to make sure that everyone on your team is aware of these profiles. As a result, once you have this definition, share it widely to ensure that all of your business's objectives are met.

CHAPTER III:

MAKING IMPECCABLE OFFER

A compelling and compelling offer is essential to any business and is the secret to success in any endeavor. Your chances of success increase with how well you craft the offer around whatever it is you've decided to sell, be it a product, service, or bit of information.

I would want to tell you that, at mile 18, when I ran my first marathon a few years ago, I pushed through to the finish line, but all I could think about was going forward. As I hobbled along in the final hour, I noticed a volunteer distributing fresh orange slices on the side of the road ahead of me.

I was tired, but I made sure to sit properly, take my time, and accept the gift with appreciation. Although I couldn't help but accept the offer of the fresh orange piece, even though it was free, I would have gladly paid for it if I had the money and the right attitude to strike up a discussion. A volunteer positioned herself two kilometers ahead of me, passing out Krispy Kreme donut halves. Regretfully, this offer did not thrill me or any other runner I encountered in the slightest.

I'm not a devout person. I've eaten many more donuts than I should have throughout the years. However, it was not a good idea to be on a sugar high three hours into the longest race of my life. The offer was unsatisfactory and ill-fitting for the circumstances.

It's ironic that after the 26.2-mile run, many racers would have been happy to see donuts, but none were found. Remember this if you are ever tasked with distributing doughnuts to marathon participants.

An offer you just can't refuse, A good offer is like an orange at mile eighteen.

It's the proposal of marriage from the person you've been waiting your whole life to see.

An offer you can't turn down is the $20,000 Bonderman Fellowship, which is awarded to University of Washington seniors who are about to graduate. The fellowship has some rather stringent rules. Take our money in cash, travel the world on your own, and then disappear for eight months. Additionally, remember to send us a brief email once in a while so we can inform your parents that you are still alive. If you predicted that hundreds of students apply for the fellowship every year, you would be right.

So how do you make a proposal that your target audience won't turn down?

Remember that you have to sell the products that people want to buy first. Make sure you are promoting to the right people at the right moment.

Sometimes the right people are in the wrong place at the wrong moment. Marathon runners are happy to indulge in doughnuts after the race, but not at mile 18.

Next, you take your product or service and transform it into an alluring pitch that extends an invitation.

Finding the right target market and developing their offer are the problems that most business entrepreneurs face. But the offer is really important. It sets the way for explosive corporate growth and opens the door to unrealized potential and revenues, beyond your wildest aspirations. But getting there is no simple task.

To make a strong offer, there are a few things you must know fundamentally. You need to be fully aware of who your customer is. You also need to be informed on the state of the business and your industry. Naturally, you also need to be conscious of your competitors. The greater your comprehension of those three ideas, Your chances of getting someone to accept your offer increase with its attractiveness and allure.

All things considered, there are several key components to making a compelling and enticing offer. They are all necessary. All of them need to be there if you're serious about succeeding in the business sector. If you disregard any one of these guidelines, you're essentially wasting your time and shouldn't expect to make any kind of significant progress.

On the other hand, you will succeed if you follow these guidelines and your offer will soon become saturated. The keys give the foundation; what matters is how you use them. If you take the time to understand and properly execute your offer, you'll be well on your way to becoming the dominant player in the market.

1. Be exact.

Developing a compelling offer starts with being crystal clear about what you're offering. Confusion prevents people from purchasing from you.

This is when your copywriting skills will come in handy. Make sure you develop and provide a genuinely clear and intelligible offer if you want them to buy.

The simplest way to do this is to explain and convey the purpose of your product or service in a clear and succinct manner. When responding, give specific details. Steer clear of employing wording that isn't precise in describing the offer. Make sure the title captures the attention of your target, speaks to what you're selling, and delivers on its promise. Usc dates, percentages, or figures to show the details of the deal.

2. Provide outstanding value.

In business, values are becoming less common. Although it really ought to be the other way around, most people choose to put in the least amount of labor in order to receive the greatest benefits. You ought to be very proud of all you accomplish. You can make an initial sale if you're just collecting stuff and hope to make a lot of money, but if the value isn't high enough, don't expect consistency. Plans that fall short of expectations are automatically recalled, disputed, and denied. This headache is not something you should bear. Reviews or news that is unpleasant or negative is not what we desire. If you go above and above in your endeavor to deliver exceptional value, your offer will gain momentum. Remember that rumors get around easily. Unfavorable press might also permanently destroy a business.

3. Provide a discount or an upgrade.

You must persuade your clients to make an instant purchase. You must charge more or give big discounts in order to do this. How can you enhance your offer to virtually eliminate the possibility of rejection? Consider carefully. Remember that the attention span of your prospect is really short. You can have trouble overcoming customer objections if you don't provide discounts or premium services. Offering incredibly low rates isn't the point; what matters is adding features to make the deal appealing.

4. Explain what you're offering.

Humans are inherently cynical. You have to persuade individuals to take advantage of your offer regardless of who you are or what you're trying to sell. Regardless of whether you've built a solid rapport with this person over time, you'll need to provide a compelling argument for your offer.

What should one offer prospective clients?

After you receive it, what do you get? It's not hard, but careful communication is needed. The language should be both fully detailed and extremely clear, as said in the first criterion. Make use of highlights that capture the psyche of the customer.

monetary proposal, Here, you want to persuade people to purchase what you're selling, not scam them.

5. A timely response is necessary.

Request prompt answers from prospective clients. The concept of scarcity needs to be considered in this case. It's possible that the deal will expire in a few hours or days. There can be a limit to the amount sold. or possibly something entirely different.

Whatever it is, it needs to be addressed right away. Emphasize the gravity of the situation. Since you won't see them again after they depart. Why, in your opinion, is the auto salesperson attempting to rush your purchase? They are aware that your prospects of closing the deal are significantly diminished the moment you go.

6. Include a strong call to action

There should be an obvious call to action in your proposal. Inform prospective clients of the action you would like them to take. Consider them as 10-year-olds who require guidance on their next course of action. This is most likely what you've seen in some of the most convincing deals that instruct you on what to do next.

For instance, click the green "Buy Now" button, complete the form, and get the product downloaded. or something like. Employ bold, huge buttons and colors, and keep the amount of clickable content on your page to a minimum. Remember that you should steer potential customers in the appropriate way and limit the number of options available to them. The offer page's menu and navigation should be eliminated for the same reason.

7. Make a firm guarantee

Provide a strong, risk-free promise to prospective clients in order to succeed and sell automatically. Prospects will take action if they think there is no risk. This explains why a 30-day money-back guarantee is included with practically all orders. Astute marketers recognize the significance of these assurances. All you need to do is transfer the client's risk to you. This demonstrates your degree of assurance that customers will be pleased with everything you have to offer.

CHAPTER IV

APPROACHING WITH ADVERTISING MEDIA IN

Advertising tells strangers about your products. You will sell more products if more people are aware of what you have to offer. You will earn more money if you sell more goods. Marketing enables you to make money off of a mediocre product. This means that even with low sales, you can still make money. It lets you make a lot of money even when you make multiple blunders.

Simply said, possessing this skill provides you countless opportunities to get it right, but bear in mind that there aren't many second chances.

For companies of all sizes, social media marketing is an effective way to connect with potential clients and customers. People find, research, follow, and purchase companies on social media, therefore you're missing out if you're not on Facebook, Instagram, LinkedIn, and other platforms!

Effective social media marketing may propel your company to new heights by creating brand advocates and increasing leads and sales.

Specifically, what is social media marketing?

A type of digital marketing known as "social media marketing" makes use of the widespread use of social media networks to accomplish branding and marketing objectives. It is more complicated than just setting up company accounts and publishing content anytime you want. Social media marketing necessitates a flexible approach with quantifiable objectives, such as:

Updating and keeping up your profiles: employing images, videos, tales, and live streaming to establish your brand and appeal to a certain audience. Pay attention to your reputation and reply to likes, shares, and comments. Follow and establish connections with customers, influencers, and followers to create a brand community.

Paid social media advertising is an additional facet of social media marketing that enables you to pay to place your business in front of a sizable audience of highly targeted customers.

Social Media Marketing's Benefits

Social media is one of the most effective free marketing channels out there right now because of its wide application and adaptability.

Make your business more human: Social networking can help your business get more involved in your industry. You may build an approachable persona that your audience can get to know, relate to, and trust through your profile, posts, and user interactions.

attract traffic: Social media is a terrific way to attract traffic to your website and convert visitors into purchases. You can do this by using your profile link, blog post, links in your articles, and advertisements. Indirect SEO factors could include social signals.

Create customers and leads: By making use of features like Instagram and Facebook stores, direct messaging, call-to-action buttons on profiles, and appointment booking possibilities, you can also use these platforms to create customers and leads.

Boost brand recognition: Since social media platforms are primarily visual, you may use this to build your visual identity and reach a wide audience. increased brand awareness correlates with increased success in all other endeavors.

Create connections: You may network, get comments, have conversations, and communicate with your fans directly through these platforms through both direct and indirect channels of communication.

Your marketing goals will be easier to accomplish the larger and more active your social media audience is.

Details regarding social media advertising

Don't just take our word for it on the advantages listed above. Take a look at some statistics on social media marketing that show how successful it is:

The average adult in America uses social media for 2.25 hours a day.

More than 70% of individuals who have a positive social media interaction with a company will recommend that company to their networks.

An average of twelve Facebook ads are clicked by users per month.

81% use Instagram as a resource for product and service research.

Almost eighty percent of Twitter users say they have a better impression of a firm after receiving a response to their tweet.

Four to five people share decisions about business on LinkedIn.

46% of TikTok users don't have any outside interruptions and are totally engrossed in the app.

What makes a social media marketing plan effective

Understand your audience by being aware of the platforms they use, the times and reasons they use them, the material they want to watch, the people they follow, and other details.

What point about your brand do you want to make clear to your audience? What emotions do you want visitors to experience after viewing your content?

material strategy: While there is room for spontaneity on social media, establishing a recognizable voice and consistently producing high-caliber material necessitate a well-defined plan.

Analytics: You can use quantitative data to inform your strategy by determining who to target, what to share, when to post, and other details.

Social media is a platform that operates in real time. If you want to use it to expand your business, you have to track trends, reply to comments, monitor engagements with your brand, publish often, and maintain your profiles.

On social media, avoid pitching your business, and advise inbound marketing. Put your attention on uplifted others around you and add value with pertinent and engaging content. Afterwards, this will organically promote your company, and others will do it for you.

creating a strategy for social media marketing

Now that you have a firm understanding of the fundamentals, it is time to implement your social media marketing plan. Your plan delineates your approach to social media marketing. It will give structure to your efforts and allow you to monitor your progress and ensure that your resources are being used effectively. This article explains how to create a social media marketing plan.

Selecting the platforms you use

Make your selection based on bandwidth, well-liked platforms in your sector, and your target market. Avoid taking on more platforms than you are able to handle efficiently. You can always start with one and increase the number as you get more accustomed to them.

Establish short-term, task-oriented goals and objectives, like making your profiles, blogging once a day for a month, or conducting a competitive analysis. With a routine in place and some information obtained, you may set more targeted and strategic goals, like increasing your following by X% or delivering X [types of material your audience like] on a monthly basis.

Report and adjust often: To find out who your audience is, what posts get the most interaction, and whether you are gaining new followers, use the analytics offered by each platform population. Expand and make use of what works, and eliminate what doesn't.

How to Begin Social Media Promotion

The hardest aspect of any marketing campaign is usually getting started. But after you've completed these easy steps, you ought to have the courage to enter!

1. Identify the market that you want to reach.

As with any marketing approach, you have to ensure that you have a complete understanding of your target population. To obtain a notion of what might work, look at analytics from current platforms, conduct market research, and use your present client data. This will assist you once you know who to target, what to target them with, and when to target them. Once you begin running your ads and gathering data, you will have even more precise information about who is seeing and reacting to your advertisement.

2. Select a single channel to begin.

It's imperative to have a cross-channel marketing plan, but you need to get proficient with the platforms first. Depending on who your target demographic is, Facebook is usually a good place to start.

3. Select some overarching objectives.

What do you hope to accomplish with your social media ads? In this case, setting SMART objectives is not necessary because it won't be feasible to determine precise measurements until you start. Still, you can usually get a sense of

which marketing target, for instance, awareness, lead generation, or conversions you'll start with.

4. Pay attention to the benchmarks

The amount you pay for social media ads will depend on a number of things, including your industry, audience, optimization plan, and other considerations, but it's always a good idea to have an idea of the approximate cost before you begin so you can set some financial objectives.

5. Employ the resources available to you.

There are a ton of free materials available, such as tutorials and roundups, to assist you with social media advertising.

6. Just get going

If you're a small business trying to start up, start small and learn as you go. The earlier you start advertising, the sooner you can begin obtaining the information the platform requires to truly optimize your ads because it takes time to become proficient with social media advertising platforms.

Ideas for promoting on social media

Are you ready to begin promoting your brand on social media?

To get you started, consider these social media marketing suggestions.

Create a range of material.

As with other facets of internet marketing, content is king when it comes to social media marketing. Make sure you regularly update your content and offer engaging, helpful content that your prospective customers will find valuable.

This covers things like how-tos and quick advice.

Information and analysis on regional and business news

Surveys, questions, and contests

Updates and announcements

It also means making use of all the different formats that are accessible on social media, including images, videos, stories, live broadcasts, online stores, and more.

Retain uniformity

Your business can promote its brand image across various social media channels by using social media for marketing. Even while every platform has its own atmosphere and voice, your business's core identity whether it's amiable, entertaining, or reliable should never change.

Engage rather than just share.

In other words, don't plan all of your postings by simply checking in once a month. Social media platforms have communities. Keep an eye on who is interacting with your content and react accordingly by leaving likes, sharing, and comments on their posts, hosting live broadcasts, putting up polls and questions to spark discussions, and reposting other people's writing.

Utilize tools for content development

If someone claims that Instagram is the most aesthetically pleasing social media network, you shouldn't believe them. They're all of them! If you want your posts to catch someone's attention on their feed, you should pair them with eye-catching artwork, photos, graphics, or artistically rendered text. Content creation services such as Canva and Freepik offer templates and capabilities that make it easy to quickly create images that are consistent with your brand, look professional, and incorporate your logo.

Because social media is a busy space, you need to consistently offer excellent content if you want to establish a following with your audience. The key to making this happen?

The three Rs stand for recycle, reuse, and repost.

Repurpose: Turn a case study into an Instagram customer spotlight, a blog article into a sequence of tweets, a webinar deck into a LinkedIn carousel post, and a Facebook post into a customer review. Numerous options are available.

Repost: This is a great way to fill in any holes in your content calendar, but it should only be done seldom. On Instagram, retweet and repost content created by users and influencers. Additionally, you can gather information from reliable sources and incorporate connections to those sources into your posts.

Recycle: Add your Facebook Live recordings to your YouTube channel, re-share your best blog posts once a month to attract new followers, and upload your TikTok and Instagram Reels.

Commence prioritizing your social media marketing strategy.

Enhancing site traffic and reach is not the only benefit of using social media for marketing. It lends your business a personality that allows customers to interact and relate to you on a deeper level.

Regardless of the platforms you use or how you use them, the most crucial thing to keep in mind is that social media is not the place to pitch your company. It's a place where you can be who you are, show off your morals, share vital information, and support those around you. People will follow you and promote your work naturally, so pitching won't be necessary. And by employing this tactic, you will accomplish all of the intangibles that lead to satisfaction and fulfillment in addition to your business goals.

CHAPTER V

NURTURING EXISTING AND QUALIFYING LEADS.

What distinguishes nurturing from lead nurturing and customer nurturing? Let's define "nurturing" in the context of marketing before delving into the operation of lead nurturing. "Nurture" may refer to "educate," "grow," "nourish," "nurture," or simply "care." There is always the idea of "encouraging the development of something" in order to progress or promote it.

Creating a marketing relationship with prospective clients who aren't quite ready to buy in order to boost their chances of conversion is known as lead nurturing. The goal of consumer education is to transform "loyal customers" from "customers." Customer care is the responsibility of the customer service team. Taking care of customers is an ongoing endeavor. This is due to the fact that interactions with clients continue even after they develop a strong sense of loyalty.

On the contrary!

	Nurturing	
	Lead Nurturing (or prospect)	**Customer Nurturing** (aka Customer Success
Goal	Convert to Paid Customer	Convert to Loyal Custome
Customer Lifecycle Stages	'Visitor' to 'Customer'	'Customer' to 'Loyal Custom
Responsibilities	Marketing	Customer Success

The art of nurturing involves developing a fruitful conversation with your prospects (Lead Nurturing) or customers (Customer Nurturing) at every stage of a person's life cycle, including visitors, prospects, users, customers, active customers, and devoted customers.

Putting a nurturing plan into action is essential to the growth and sustainability of your business. All communications with potential clients or customers are regarded as nurturing endeavors.

Lead nurturing is the main topic of this tutorial. But first, it was important to define "nurturing," "lead nurturing," and "customer nurturing," as well as their respective roles.

The function of lead scoring in lead nurturing

Now let's examine lead scoring. The technique of assigning scores to prospects based on their behavioral data and profile is known as lead scoring.Lead scoring and converting prospects into customers go hand in hand since lead nurturing is an ongoing dialogue (or contact) with prospects that increases the likelihood of conversion. They are beneficial to each other.

Lead scoring helps marketing evaluate the effectiveness of nurturing campaigns and sales prioritize leads.

Your lead scoring and nurturing tactics will change based on where your business is in its development. Depending on the stage of development of your company, lead scoring is more or less applicable. To keep things simple, we can categorize the growth of a company into three stages:

The Product–Market Fit search is related to the seed phase. Creating a workable service or product that will act as "proof" of concept is the company's aim.

the expansion phase, during which the business gains market share and attracts new clients.

the mature stage at which the business focuses on making its offering as good as it can be.

More specifically, lead scoring is not the main priority in the seed stage. If you just produce two or three leads per day, you do not need to score your leads.

Nevertheless, it can be beneficial to start with a simple grading scheme. This can assist you in learning more about the buying processes of your prospects. You can expedite the process of optimizing your lead scoring system once you enter the growth phase, since you will have access to previous data spanning several months or years.

Track as many user actions on your product as you can initially. This can help you identify the behavioral patterns associated with the highest conversion rates and establish statistical relationships.

Lead scoring becomes quite useful as your user base is expanding. Establishing a grading system to separate prospects with a specific pain point from those who need to be educated about the problems and their solutions (also known as "nurtured" or "warmed up") becomes crucial when you receive dozens, if not hundreds, of leads per day.

At this point, scoring is essential to maximizing your resource utilization.

As your business expands, lead nurturing might go from general correspondence to more targeted correspondence based on profile segmentation. Create unique automatic situations for every profile. For instance, the company might be tempted to send everyone the same batch of automated emails if a prospect joins up during the priming period.

The business may decide to start several different campaigns throughout the expansion stage, targeting different audiences such as financial prospects, influencers, decision-makers, and so on. Separating communications can be done according to the roles, industries, and needs of the prospects.

By the last, mature phase, companies should have procedures in place for lead scoring and lead nurturing that are reliable and tested. The company now has a sufficient amount of data to build robust models and further segment its advertising.

"Pain" and "Fit" are a pair. The results of this study apply to both incoming and outgoing leads. But in both instances, the pattern is different:

We start with the Fit in outbound and progress towards the discomfort. After a product is mass-marketed, the company ascertains whether the leads actually have the issue that the solution resolves.

Conversely, inbound starts with the discomfort and moves toward the fit. Put differently, the prospect has identified a problem for which he needs a solution and has found the company as a result. The business must then qualify the lead and determine if it is a good fit.

A Lead Scoring system's core component is the Fit / Pain pair.

Let's review the purpose of lead scoring, which is to help the company prioritize leads, increase conversion rates, and shorten sales cycles, before getting into the details of the different scoring methods.

Numerous studies show that salespeople only devote around one-third of their time to doing what they do bestselling to and interacting with clients and prospects.

Lead scoring increases sales productivity by concentrating on the most valuable prospects over time. Setting priorities helps the company use its resources more efficiently. Salespeople provide prospects with a genuine chance of converting extra time.

The more inbound leads there are, the more important lead scoring becomes. Actually, it is best to give inbound leads precedence over outgoing leads.

Simply put, lead scoring is a marketing tactic based on a scientific procedure that evaluates fit and pain. The answers to the next two queries are given.

What "pain" does the prospect have that our solution claims to solve? In light of the prospect's other ongoing worries and difficulties, how serious is this issue?

Does this potential customer "fit" with our target market? Do they have enough money to buy our product? Do they possess the internal resources necessary to implement the product within their company?

A concise summary of the complete lead scoring system development process is to identify the organization's definitions of "fit" and "pain." The score indicates the lead's issue and how well the prospect fits your target population based on the behavioral data at your disposal.

How Can I Establish a System for Scoring Leads?

The most common method for establishing a lead scoring system is to give each lead a number, and then divide the leads into three or four categories according to the scores they receive: A, B, C, D, or "Warm," "Cold," and/or "Hot." As an example, you might have:

Leads with a score of 100 or above are ready to be forwarded to sales.

B Leads are classified as 75-99 Leads.

50–74 Leads is the range of C Leads.

D = Fewer than fifty points

The issue with this conventional method is that, whereas A leads are universally understood to be hot leads that are ready to be passed to the sales department, there is sometimes little consensus regarding the differences between B, C, and D leads. So, we suggest a more straightforward taxonomy that consists of just two categories:

Leads that are prepared for sales, or SDR-ready

leads that are not yet in the transmission process.

Numerical numbers can then be used based on their maturity level to identify leads that aren't ready to move further. From our vantage point, category scoring is not nearly as significant as numerical score. It makes far more in-depth examination possible.

What precisely is a mature lead (ready for SDR)?

A lead is deemed mature and prepared for a salesperson to approach after it reaches a certain level of fit and breadth. If lead scoring is new to you, you'll need to ascertain which behaviors and actions lead a prospect to make a purchase. Your mature lead definition should ideally be linked to a conversion rate of between 10% and 15%. This suggests that 10–15% of prospects that go to the SDR-ready stage actually make a purchase.

You have to iteratively test and improve your model in order to maximize your SDR-ready. The sales team's capacity to handle a certain workload will determine how far along the maturity level should be. The relationship between the target score (maturity score) and the predicted conversion rate must be understood. Setting a low conversion barrier (8–10%) could cause your team to spend time qualifying leads that won't become customers. On the other side, raising the maturity barrier (15–20%) calls for a longer lead nurturing procedure. The first option adds to the salesperson's effort, while the second adds to the marketing team's workload. Every organization has a different maturity criterion at which a lead qualifies. There isn't just one rule. Each business should continuously revise this threshold as testing and experience mount.

What elements are used when determining the score?

Returning to our equation, let's: Fit Score + Pain Score equals Lead Score.

For a lead scoring approach to be effective, two types of data must be used:

Profile and demographic information, to ensure the fit

behavioral information to define the pain

Demographic statistics about the profile

The demographic data, also known as a profile, is globally static information that is utilized as soon as a prospect joins your CRM or marketing automation platform. The top five B2B demographics are as follows:

The email: It is up to you to decide if the address is commercial or personal. Since a business address suggests that the prospect is keen to engage with you on a corporate level, email addresses should be given greater weight.

The circumstances: You can find this information online, by asking your prospects, or by using a contact list optimization service. The higher the prospect's standing in the organizational hierarchy of the corporation, the higher their score. But the prospect's standing within the company serves purposes beyond simple rating. It helps ascertain the prospect's level of engagement with the buying process. It is advised that you create a different email sequence for every end user, decision maker, influencer, and status. We will talk about this topic again later.

The organization: Knowing the exact name of the company is crucial as it will reveal whether or not it falls inside your target market. You can award the possibility a higher score if it is.

Where: This is a crucial component because not many businesses offer their goods internationally. Regardless of whether your company does, not every market is the same or has the same potential. Therefore, it goes without saying that location can be used to score.

Dimensions:A key indicator of a company's potential earnings and purchasing power is its size. Generally speaking, the company's total size is not the most crucial element. For instance, it could be helpful to know the size of the sales department if you sell a SaaS solution for salespeople.

Depending on the business and the marketed product, each of these characteristics will have a different level of significance and weight. The scoring will be impacted by the disparity in their weighting.

Information about behavior

Finding profile data and using it for scoring is not too difficult. Behavioral data is much harder to find and use.

First of all, behavioral considerations outweigh demographic criteria by a wide margin. Secondly, behavioral data is dynamic by nature. It has to be updated frequently. Moreover, there aren't many third-party solutions available for scoring analyses of behavioral data. Some tools measure how users interact with your product, but only your employees are able to correlate user behavior with conversion rate.

Two categories of behavioral data exist.

Information about how prospects use the product is contained in engagement data related to product consumption. This is the most important behavioral data point by far. Conversion probability and product usage are closely related.

Commitment information irrelevant to the use of the product, like:

Get the white paper in copy form.

Attend a webinar.

The knowledge base, the FAQ, the price list page...

Even the smallest actions, like visiting a website, opening an email, clicking a link in an email, and so on, shouldn't be given a score. These behaviors rarely indicate a prospect's interest in the product and require very little from them. These behaviors rarely indicate a prospect's interest in the product and require very little from them. Most of the time, their only driving force is curiosity

As soon as your business is operational, we advise you to put in place a mechanism for tracking user-product interactions. This will provide you access to historical data when creating your lead scoring system.

When you get the SDR-ready Score, what happens next?

The transfer from marketing to sales should be as smooth as possible once your leads are SDR-ready. One factor in lead management de-qualification is time. Making a rule that requires salespeople to get in touch with SDR-ready leads within X hours is a smart approach. 48 hours, for example.

Three categories can be used to classify the SDR-ready leads after the sales force has qualified them:

The potential does fit the requirements, yes. They go into the funnel for sales. They either convert (lead => customer) or they don't. These two situations are as follows. He moves from lead nurturing to customer nurturing if he converts. Onboarding campaigns may be initiated.

Include the prospect in your "Product Engagement" campaign if he doesn't convert. This potential client might eventually turn into a customer. We can't ignore them.

It doesn't mean that a prospect will never buy just because they don't buy right away.

Maybe the candidate isn't qualified enough. In terms of fit (they fit your target audience), they can be qualified, but not in terms of pain (their need is not consistent enough), or vice versa. In this case, you could start a conversation with these leads by emailing them frequently with goal-oriented content. Later on, we will go more into the nature and substance of campaigns.

No, there is little chance of a conversion. They don't have enough credentials in terms of pain and fit. This doesn't mean you can't score them or send them email campaigns; if they choose to convert, they will do so on their own.

The final group poses a fundamental query: how can leads whose needs fluctuate and do not align with the company's intended clientele wind up in

the hands of sales? In terms of lead score, how do they know they've advanced past the maturity level? There are several choices. A rival, a student, or an investor who has researched your idea may be the lead. But if this keeps happening, your lead scoring system is probably having issues. You need to clearly modify your lead scoring technique if more than 5 percent of the leads that are forwarded on to sales are in the "will never convert" category.

The top four lead scoring mistakes that occur

Particularly in SaaS companies, lead nurturing and lead scoring are essential elements of B2B strategy. Still, not many companies get it right. The following are the top four lead scoring errors:

The first mistake is not keeping an eye on how your leads are using your website or product.

Once more, you shouldn't put off tracking. You should anticipate and start collecting data on your prospects' behavior in your product or on your website immediately, even if you are a start-up with few leads. You can use this to help design your lead scoring system.

Error #2: Making the lead scoring system too complicated.

Acknowledge upfront that you will never be able to design the ideal Lead Scoring model from the beginning. Therefore, the best approach is to start small and make small adjustments to the model, weights, data, and metrics as needed.

Avoid using a category rating system (A, B, C, D, etc.). This further muddles and complicates matters. It is a waste of time to argue over whether a lead is B or C.

Error #3: Making an excessive number of indicator attempts.

No more than 20 to 25 engagement indicators should be scored in order to prevent your scoring system from getting unduly complicated. We advise utilizing ten to fifteen indicators at first. You can get rid of signals that affect the conversion rate by less than X% by mentioning the percentage in issue. The objective is to include elements and actions in the total score computation that significantly affect the conversion of leads into consumers.

Error #4: Dependent upon intuition

Most firms overvalue important features based on intuition and experience. You must put aside your intuition and choose your indications based on statistical analysis, even basic analysis, in order to create an effective lead scoring system.

The key automatic situations that will warm up your leads

We'll discuss pre-written email sequences that are sent out automatically in this part based on triggers. You may improve fit and bread qualification, nurture leads, and boost prospects' engagement with your offerings by implementing these steps.

Scheduled email messages are the first step in lead nurturing. Although most marketers are familiar with automated scripts, they are often underutilized in terms of their potential for lead scoring and lead nurturing.We'll also examine how segmentation could improve the effectiveness of your campaigns.

What constitutes a basic automated scenario example?

a series of emails that are sent to a potential customer within the first week or two of the product's free trial period. In this instance, it is a "welcome" circumstance.

Since it deals with your prospects' first interactions with you, this is unquestionably the most important case. An additional illustration would be the series of emails sent following a transaction, the first of which is usually an order confirmation email.

Eight situations for lead engagement that are automatable

1. Welcome-Visitor Campaigns

The goal of this scenario is to complete a prospect's registration for a service and to educate them on the primary benefits of your product so that they desire to move further. Here's an example of an email chain:

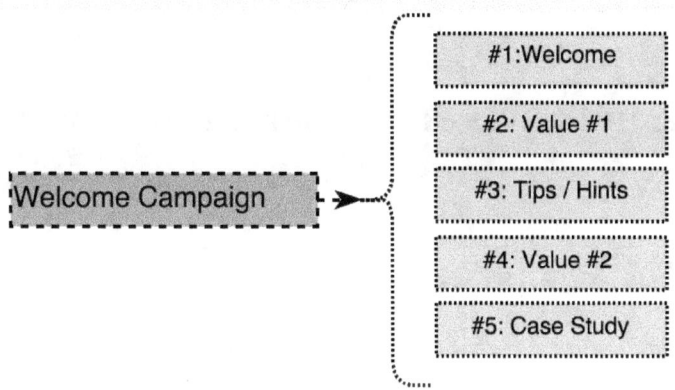

Once the prospect becomes an active user, you can, of course, end the process at that point. This series introduces your value offer to your prospect. Teaching your prospect everything they need to know about your product to ensure they get the most out of it is the next step.

2. Initiatives for onboarding new users

The second email series aims to support the prospect in their first steps and motivate them to use the product.

The onboarding campaign teaches users how to get the most out of the product by filling out forms or using the program's early steps, while the welcome campaign explains why using the product is worthwhile. Let's examine a few particular instances. An email welcoming the user to LinkedIn is issued upon signup.

Following registration, users will receive a series of welcome letters urging them to visit LinkedIn again if they do not log in to their account. If a user has signed up for LinkedIn and is using the service, but has not finished filling out all of the information relevant to their profile, LinkedIn will now start the onboarding process. These emails provide them with an explanation of why and how updating their profile would make better use of LinkedIn.

3. Initiatives for the upbringing of

In this scenario, the objective is to convince a lead to sample a product or turn them into a mature lead (SDR-ready).

Not every potential customer will visit the free trial page on your website. Offering digital content, such as research, case studies, or white papers, is another way to get a prospect to sign up for your trial period.

Depending on the cycle of sales and the type of your product, nurturing campaigns can aim for two things:

If you are offering a free trial period, then more people will sign up for it.

Get prospects to the maturity score (which results in a handover from marketing to sales) if you do not offer a free trial period.

4. Initiatives aimed at boosting product interaction

Increasing your prospects' level of involvement and keeping them coming back to the product is the aim of this kind of scenario. For a SaaS business using a freemium business model, this is a crucial situation. Businesses who adopt this tactic have to make sure that users who aren't paying for the product use it and do so more often.

5. Brand-new marketing initiatives to attract customers

Users who have recently joined up for a paying offer are the target audience for this scenario. Establishing a connection between the Customer Success team and new, paying customers is the aim. This program is designed to keep customers.

The goal of these emails is to help the new customer get the most out of the product. For example, to help the user integrate the tool with other platforms or services. In situations like this, you can recommend training, webinars, tutorials, support team appointments, and so on.

6. Campaigns to upsell

In these situations, the objective is to notify the customer about new features, modules, services, or premium goods in an effort to get them to upgrade to a more expensive subscription plan.

7. Renewal campaigns

Notifying the customer that their subscription is about to expire and convincing them to renew it are the objectives here.

Transactional emails

Last but not least, remember email sequences sent in a transactional setting. Don't forget to include transactional scenarios in your lead nurturing toolkit. These may be emails urging consumers to download bills, change their passwords, check their email, and so forth.

In conclusion, creating too many lead categories, scoring too many items, and delaying starting user behavior tracking are the most frequent mistakes made while scoring leads.

With automated scenario-based email marketing, you may gradually increase your audience's engagement with your product.

Above all, segmenting your emails gradually will increase their efficacy and, consequently, your performance metrics.

CHAPTER VI

DISTRIBUTING LEADS TO YOUR SALES TEAM IN

Your marketing department is typically in charge of lead generation, or the first lead generation process. Once you obtain those leads, however, you'll need the sales team to turn them into customers.

If your company is like most others, you have a number of agents in your sales team, each of whom is in charge of a specific lead or client. You have the option of giving your sales representatives random leads to work with. Still, it's usually better to have an effective lead distribution process in place.

Referring prospects to sales departments

If you're trying to distribute leads around your sales staff, you might not know how to accomplish it. When deciding which salespeople should be given which leads, what variables should you take into account?

1. Respond to leads right away

One of the first things to get right when handling leads is responding quickly. If a lead shows interest in meeting with you or becoming a client, you don't want to let them down.

What justifies a discussion on it?Because it can be easy to wait too long when attempting to decide how best to allocate a lead, which may cause the lead to become disinterested or to choose an opponent.

If you want to keep leads, you have to get back to them as soon as possible. This involves sending leads to the sales team as soon as possible. This is why you shouldn't pressure yourself to choose a choice every time you have to route a lead. Rather, implement a system that allows you to forward leads as soon as they are received.

2. Consider the position of your leads within the funnel.

Every lead is unique. Some are almost ready to buy from you right then, while others are still unsure about doing business with you. Depending on where a lead is in the sales funnel, you may want to allocate them to a different sales team or representative.

This is important because treating a middle-of-the-funnel lead like a bottom-of-the-funnel lead, or vice versa, usually won't go over well. You risk wasting their time by telling them stuff they've previously heard, or you risk pressuring them into buying before they're ready.

Ensuring that leads receive the right kind of sales treatment involves assigning them to a sales person after figuring out where they are in the funnel.

3. Select the best-performing sales model.

A lot of businesses, particularly small ones, just have one sales team that handles all of their leads and clients.

That may have a significant effect on your business.

But different products or services often require different approaches to selling them. This is the reason why some companies have different sales teams, or different departments within a single team, that use different sales methods. If it describes you, consider which team should receive each lead. For example, you might give tech help and sell computer equipment at the same time. Since your products and services would inevitably require fairly diverse sales methods, you may have distinct salespeople and possibly even completely different pipelines for them.

In that scenario, when a lead expressing interest in your products materializes, be sure you assign them to a representative that specializes in product sales as opposed to consulting.

4. Assign jobs to the most qualified delegates.

Although they have been discussed in passing a few times already, sales representatives nevertheless have advantages and disadvantages that should be considered.

Representatives may possess diverse specializations or expertise working with different types of clients, which makes them especially suitable for specific leads.

Imagine that you offer metal fabrication services, and you receive a new lead from an aircraft manufacturer. You could theoretically provide that lead to any one of your sales agents. But after thinking about each salesperson, you realize that Brent is particularly skilled at closing deals with aircraft manufacturers.

It makes sense to believe that Brent will be particularly skilled at turning this lead in light of that information. This is probably an excellent reason to give him that lead.

5. Make use of lead scoring

Periods of low lead volume may happen from time to time. That being said, there are times when you may get too many leads at once. When that happens, you should forward them to your sales team in a more critical sequence; lead scoring can help you do so. You give each lead a number throughout the lead scoring process that represents their importance in terms of priority. That value may be established based on variables like geography or the amount of money you expect to make if they become a customer.

To make sure you get the most money out of every lead, you can then allocate the highest scoring leads first, and then the lowest.   Lead handoff can be difficult, but it can be made much easier if you have a clear process, the right tools, and a firm understanding of how your team can use fit and engagement activities to qualify leads. More importantly, it also becomes considerably more effective. With your sales and marketing teams in charge of development, these stages will help you create a customized lead handoff procedure for your business. They will ensure that the solution they come up with meets their needs.

CHAPTER VII

PROVIDING A WORLD-CLASS EXPERIENCE IN

84% of consumers believe that customer service is one of the most crucial factors to take into account when deciding whether or not to purchase from a company, according to Zendesk. This figure highlights the tremendous value of providing world-class service as well as the need of providing at least competent customer service. It proves that your bottom line can be greatly impacted by the caliber of your customer service. If your finest marketing and sales strategies aren't supported by first-rate customer care, they won't last very long. Furthermore, the benefits and effect of first-rate service extend beyond the company. They may grow beyond your present clientele, which makes the strategy a useful tool in and of itself for attracting new clients.

Your business can establish a reputation as a committed entity that puts its customers first if it consistently and continuously strives to provide world-class service. Prospects will always respect a company that they believe will respect them back.

Our lives and career paths are shaped by our experiences. Over the years, I've collaborated with a range of leaders, taking use of their guidance, camaraderie, and expertise to create enduring, unforgettable experiences for partners, clients, and myself.

Let's also take a closer look at how company executives will be affected by the new experience economy.

The Value of Human Contact

I had carefully thought out the places I wanted to see in Southern Spain this summer. A few days before our trip, we decided to stay an extra day in Seville. After exchanging a few emails, the hotel receptionist verified our request for an additional day.

The receptionist informed us that she was unable to confirm the additional day since she had not noticed it in the reservation system when we arrived in Sevilla. This was not a fun way to start our holiday. In addition to verifying our availability for the extra day, she promptly looked into other options and upgraded us to a large room at no additional cost.

Within a few minutes, we received a nice TripAdvisor feedback with "5 Stars". As opposed to placing the blame on the reservation system, the receptionist responded to our request "in the moment."

Another family approached the reception desk, appearing upset, while we waited for the suite to be ready. I couldn't help but overhear a similar conversation, in which the reservation system accurately reflected their booking. It's evident that there was a systemic problem with the hotel reservation system. In situations like these, having a human touch that is, receptionist assistance is crucial to maintaining a top-notch experience.

Gaining the Hearts and Minds of Others

Businesses need to prepare for "longer term strategic improvements" in addition to meeting "in-the-moment" objectives in order to deliver exceptional customer and employee experiences.

Bain & Company uses the "inner Loop and Outer Loop" approach. The hotel receptionist in the aforementioned situation did a fantastic job of "responding in the moment" and attending to the needs of the hotel guests. However, this tactic can result in missed opportunities for money if the reservation system's flaws are not fixed.

Companies need to be proactive in finding ways to close experience gaps by merging operational data such as reservation system transactions—with consumer experience data, like TripAdvisor reviews. This requires combining operational data on "What is the Return on Investment" (O-data) with user feedback on "How One Feels" (X-data).

Business executives may find these insights useful in reevaluating their operations and business structures. By doing so, they will be able to better respond to requests that arise "in the moment" and carry out the investment plan for "longer term strategic improvements," all the while winning over more supporters and supporters.

CHAPTER VIII

INCREASING THE LIFETIME VALUE OF CUSTOMER IN

While getting new clients is always wonderful, which ones are the biggest drivers of your income growth?

Which customer spends $1000 all at once, or the one who regularly spends $50 over several years?

As it happens, a customer who makes little, regular purchases over time ends up making more money than a person who splurges on a deal once and never comes back. It is therefore advantageous for your customer success and marketing teams to focus on keeping these kinds of high-value consumers. But how are you supposed to judge which of those customers are worth it?

The Customer Lifetime Value (CLV) figure is useful in this situation. Your target audience's level of satisfaction with your product or service, areas for improvement to gain their loyalty, and the amount of money you should set aside for customer retention marketing can all be ascertained by measuring CLV.

This chapter will define CLV, provide an efficient calculation method, and discuss the importance of monitoring for all subscription businesses.

Customer Lifetime Value (CLV), What does it mean?

The total predictable revenue that a business can get from a paying client over the length of their lifetime is known as client Lifetime Value, or CLV.

A customer's lifetime is one year, for instance, if they subscribe to one of your goods under a one-year plan. Their lifetime value will be what you hope to earn that year.

Consequently, a customer's lifetime value (CLV) increases with the length of time they spend with you and the frequency of their purchases. You can leverage the customer profiles that provide the highest customer lifetime value (CLV) to attract new, high-value clients who fit in with those already.

What does your subscription business stand to gain by evaluating Customer Lifetime Value?

Identify high-value clients

Companies don't want to spend time or money on unprofitable customer acquisition. They're curious about the optimal amount of

money to spend on marketing in order to draw in the most customers. But what does 'Best Customer' mean to them specifically? There are several ways to react to this: The simplest to get and retain as well as the most profitable and devoted customers. And what about the others? High-value customers are those who have a high Customer Lifetime Value (CLV). By figuring out each customer's CLV and ranking them according to the findings, you may identify high-value clients. A consumer is more valuable if their CLV is higher. In order to increase the likelihood of acquiring and keeping such high-value customers, you can adjust your marketing and sales strategies and develop your product with knowledge by evaluating CLV.

Decide how much capital to invest in the purchase.

Spending more money on client acquisition than you do on retention is the surest way to suffocate a business. Understanding the relationship between your CLV and your Customer Acquisition Cost is therefore crucial. client lifetime value (CLV) represents the value of a client, whereas cost of acquisition (CAC) represents the other side of the equation. The ultimate question, "What is the true value of a customer to my business?" is answered by the balanced ratio of these two indications. When combined, the metrics CAC and CLV offer a model Return On Investment (ROI) that a business could receive from gaining a customer. This model helps determine whether the investment levels are sustainable for long-term value development and economic viability.

Let's use the example of a subscription box company to examine the relationship between CLV and CAC. Let's say they provide their goods in three distinct methods: Costs for small, medium, and big boxes range from $8 to $21.

The revenue from a customer who orders fifteen boxes annually for eight years on average is $1800 [(8+16+21)/3 * 15 boxes * 8 years = $1800].

In order to receive $1800 from clients, the business must first seek out and bring on new clients. Each month, they spend roughly $7500 on acquiring new customers.

Their CAC is $75 ($7500/100) since they spend $75 on each customer. The extra costs that the business incurs annually for each customer total $30.

Accordingly, a customer's CLV (as calculated above) is $1800 with the business. - $30 (additional expenditures) - $80 (total CAC: 8 years * $10/year) = $1690.

This indicates that during the length of the business's eight-year relationship, the average customer is worth $1690 in earnings. We can infer that the business is making good use of its marketing budget because each client will bring in more revenue than it spent on acquisition, as seen by the CAC of $75 being less than the CLV of $1690.

Boost consumer adherence to brands

One of the most important and challenging attributes for a business to achieve is brand loyalty. Customer connections gain a new dimension from the CLV by making firms that understand the value of their customers, especially those that are thought to be dependable and have a high CLV.

Clients that have a high lifetime value (CLV) are devoted and offer your business several advantages. They remain with your business longer and offer insightful input as it expands. These customers end up becoming your best brand ambassadors, giving you favorable word-of-mouth recommendations that have a significant impact on the growth of your business's reputation.

Therefore, focusing on raising your CLV through a variety of loyalty initiatives is essential to creating customer engagement and solidifying brand loyalty.

How is the lifetime value of a customer (CLV) determined?

The calculation of Customer Lifetime Value involves multiplying the average purchase value, frequency of purchases, and lifespan of your customers.

Step 1: To calculate the Average Purchase Value (APV), tally up all of the revenue received over a given period of time, then divide that amount by the total number of sales made during that same period. In the event if your business generated $20,000 in revenue from 200 sales in a given month, for instance, the APV would have been $100 ($20,000 / 200).

Step 2: The number of purchases divided by the total number of unique consumers yields the average purchase frequency (APF).

A consumer is only included in the computation once if they made several purchases during a specific time frame.

The annual percentage yield (APF) is equal to 200 purchases divided by 40 consumers, or five times, if your business made $20,000 from 40 customers who completed 200 transactions.

Step 3: Add together all of your clients' lifespans and divide the total by the number of clients to determine the Average Client Lifespan (ACL).The churn rate can be used to calculate

ACL if your business is new and does not have the necessary number of customers in sample.

Clients at the beginning of the period - clients at the conclusion of the period / clients at the beginning of the period

For instance, the churn rate is (50 - 45) / 50 = 0.1 if your business starts the month with 50 clients but by the end of the month, it only has 45.

The formula for calculating the Average Customer Lifespan (ACL) is 1/Churn rate = 1 / 0.1 = 10 months.

Step 4: We can just multiply all of the components together now that we have all of the ones needed for CLV.

The value of a customer's lifetime is: Given a customer lifespan of 36 months, five buy frequencies, and an average purchase value of $100, the Customer Lifetime Value may be calculated as follows: CLV on average = $100 * 5 * 36 = $18,000.

To obtain a more accurate CLV estimate, use gross margin. A CLV calculation tells you how much money you get from each customer, but not how much profit you make. Take into consideration your gross margin, or the portion of your revenue that is allocated to making additional purchases, in order to obtain a more accurate understanding of each customer's profitability.

Your gross margin is the portion of your total revenue that is left over after subtracting the cost of goods sold (COGS).

For instance, if your COGS is $8,000 and your total monthly income is $20,000, you would deduct the COGS from the revenue to obtain $20,000 - $8,000 = $12,000.

To obtain a 0.6 gross margin, divide the result by the total revenue (12,000 / 20,000 = 0.6).

Gross margin can be expressed as a percentage by multiplying 0.6 by 100 to obtain 60%.

To obtain a more realistic CLV, double the gross margin, average customer longevity, and customer value:

$500 * 36 * 0.6 = $10,800 is the CLV.

This figure is significantly less than the $18,000 we determined from the prior CLV computation, suggesting that a significant chunk of the money you get from each customer is only being used to cover the cost of the items they buy. It's important to figure out the gross margin and factor it into the CLV calculation if you want to know how much money your clients are worth in terms of funds you can use for other aspects of your business operations.

Techniques for computing CLV

There are other methods to compute CLV, despite the fact that we just saw one simple computation above. There are other approaches, such as historical, predictive, and traditional, and the best one to use will rely on the kind of business and the resources at hand.

Contextual history

A quick and simple method to determine a customer's lifetime value based on previous gross profits your company has made is to use historical CLV. All you need is information from past purchases, so the calculation is simple. Cohort analysis or average revenue per user (ARPU) can be used to compute historical CLV.

Assume that during the course of three months, 20 of your clients brought in $1,300 in revenue for your business.Your three-month ARPU is $1,300 / 20 = $65.

Let's see how much money you get in a year from these customers.

ARPU during a 12-month period equals ARPU over a 3-month period * 4 ($65 * 4 = $260 per client annually).

By combining customers who shared comparable features and made their first purchase in the same month, cohort analysis expands on the ARPU approach. If you have a large enough data collection, you may use cohort analysis to compute the average revenue for your typical client instead of calculating the average revenue for your average customer. average revenue for specific cohorts whose characteristics are critical to the forecast you are trying to construct.

The primary drawback of historical CLV is that it aggregates customers with potentially disparate buying patterns. If you're altering your products or marketing approach, this can be an issue. It's possible that recent modifications have already drawn in new customers, whose preferences and buying decisions won't be sufficiently forecasted by previous CLV. Cohort analysis can be useful in some situations since it lets you find consumer cohorts that are more likely to resemble your target market. You might find, nevertheless, that using data from previous client cohorts isn't accurately predicting your future CLV.

predicting approach

The goal of predictive CLV is to estimate the overall value that a client will bring to a business during their lifetime. Based on past transactions as well as current customer behavioral trends, including frequency of purchase, the predictive strategy is implemented. In contrast to historical CLV, which is limited to offering insights into previous events, predictive CLV may assist you in understanding a customer's current value as well as projecting how their value will grow over time. In order to attract and retain customers with a high lifetime value, this could help you prioritize your engagement and acquisition efforts and start running targeted advertising.

T: The volume of average monthly transactions

Average Order Value is referred to as AOV.   Customer lifetime average (measured in months) and average gross margin (AGM)

Now let's create some fake numbers to put into this formula.

T (Total Average Transactions):

Duration: three months

Total number of transactions: 120 T divided by 120/3 equals 40 AOV.

Ten thousand dollars in total revenue in August.

20 orders: AGM (Average Gross Margin) = $10,000 / 20 orders = $500; this yields the gross margin % for the month.

Gross Margin * 100 = [(Total Revenue - Cost of Goods Sold) / Total Revenue]

Example: $10,000 was the total revenue for August.

$8,000 is the sales cost.

$10,000 - ($8,000 - $10,000) / $10,000] * Gross Margin (%) * 100 = 33%

- Calculate the average gross margin for a three-month period.

Gross Margin Overall = 0.87

The average gross margin is equivalent to 0.29 times the Average Customer Lifespan (ALT).

ALT = 1 / Turnover Rate

To find the turnover rate, take the following actions:

Assume you had 200 clients at the start of August and 150 at the end of

September. (200 - 150) / 200 = 50 / 200 = 0.25, or 25%, will be the turnover rate.

4 months is the average customer lifetime (ALT), or 1 / 25%, or 1 / 0.25.

Having obtained all the necessary information, we can now calculate our projected CLV:

T stands for the average number of transactions.

Average Order Value (AOV) = $500 and Average Gross Margin (AGM) = 0.29

Four months is the average customer lifetime (ALT).

(T * AOV * AGM * ALT) / Total number of clients at the end of the specified time is the predicted CLV.

By the end of September, the projected CLV is (40 * $500 * 0.29 * 4) / 150 clients.

= $154.66 / (150 / 23,200).

Traditional method

A company's growth is not at all linear. What happens then if you have to account for changes that transpire during a client's lifetime and your sales per customer fluctuate year after year? In this case, a more thorough CLV computation that accounts for margins, inflation, and retention rate and provides a more detailed view of CLV increase over time is needed.

The profit you expect to make over the course of a normal client lifetime is known as gross margin contribution per customer, or GML. It is calculated as revenue less cost of goods sold.

The percentage of customers who stick with your business over an extended period of time is known as the retention rate, or R.

The discount rate, represented by the letter D, is used to account for inflation. For SaaS businesses, a 10% discount is typically applied.

For instance:

Each client's gross margin contribution (GMC) is 0.29.

Average total revenue is $1,000.

$290 is the retention rate (GML * 1,000).

Let's say you own: 300 clients at the end of the month 50 new customers were added during the month. Beginning of the month customers = 270 R = [(300 − 50) / 270] * 100 = 0.9 * 100 = 90%; * 100 = (250 / 270).

Consider the standard 10% discount rate as an illustration.

Just input the values into the CLV formula.

[R / (1 + D - R)] in GML * = CLV * [0.9 / (1+ 0.1 - 0.9)] = $290 * CLV

$1,305 is equal to $290 * (0.9 / 0.2) = $290 * 4.5.

Profitable subscription businesses evaluate their customer lifetime value on a regular basis and strive to increase it.

With CLV, companies may enhance their customer service and marketing strategies, increasing revenue and client retention. One can compute CLV in a number of methods. All of these strategies have benefits and drawbacks, and the optimal approach depends on your company's size, industry it operates in, tools it uses to create KPIs, and how much it spends on marketing and sales.

While CLV is only one component of a complicated financial puzzle, when combined with other indicators and cutting-edge analytics, it may be a useful tool for determining your customers' value and optimizing their business.

CHAPTER XI

ENHANCING

CUSTOMER RECOMMENDATIONS

A key component of customer success is using your service to create brand champions, and a customer referral program can assist.

Because they are so cheap to obtain, referrals are quite advantageous. A referral's exact value varies based on the type of business, but in general, it's equal to the client's lifetime value (LTV) plus the acquisition cost (CAC), which you can spend to acquire new customers.

In a recent survey, 94% of respondents said they would recommend a business whose service they thought was "very good." You will concur with me that you would also recommend a business whose customers rate their service as "very good." It follows that you can outsource a lot of the grunt labor to an army of contented clients.

Uncertain about how to prepare for these interactions with customers? All the information you require to establish, grow, and oversee an effective referral program is provided here.

The information tells the following tale: Companies found that compared to leads generated through other marketing channels, referred clients had a 30% higher conversion rate, a 16% higher lifetime value rate, and a 37% higher retention rate.

On the other hand, you are essentially asking your clients to act as your sales and marketing representatives.

Additionally, tact and consistency are essential when developing new business through referrals.

One kind of word-of-mouth marketing tactic that motivates clients to recommend your company is a referral program. Through referral programs, customers can tell their friends, coworkers, and partners about their brand experience instead of leaving online reviews or filling out customer feedback forms.

The purpose of a referral program is to increase your company's lead generation. You're not just letting everyone in, though.

If you encourage your customers to think of others who will benefit from your product or service, they will refer to leads that are a good fit for your firm.

These leads are not only a fantastic fit for your company, but they also know it and its reputation, which only makes it easier for your marketing and sales team to engage and nurture clients.

They were introduced by someone they know, so they have a reliable source informing them that your company is reliable and offers a satisfying customer experience.

If your business is prepared to leverage word-of-mouth marketing, keep reading for guidance on establishing a customer referral program.

1. Start by creating templates for client recommendations.

Whether you work in a multi-person referral team or are a one-person customer referral engine, templates can help you.Any employee in the organization who needs them can use them, and they can be tailored to fit the voice and tone of your brand.

You may create a database of the following using these free customer referral templates: Emails asking for recommendations, emails following up on recommendations, and social media content promoting the business's referral program. And still more.

As an alternative, refer to Referral Factory's detailed instructions.

2. Specify your goals.

Think about the benefits you hope to obtain from this referral scheme.

Are growth and revenue more at the forefront of your goals? Would you like to add retention to the mix? Do you work in a field where a great deal of trust is required?

After determining your objectives and giving them precise definitions, the next steps ought to be clear.

3. Find out how referrals are coming into your business.

Analyzing the sources and methods of referrals or whether any that come into your company is a wise place to start.

This is the point at which you should assess how marketing, sales management, support, and any other department responsible for cultivating customer relationships have historically handled referrals.

Your current location will be shown as a result.

Additionally, you want to be aware of an existing customer's worth. How many recommendations must you make in order to equal the amount of time required to oversee and manage onboarding initiatives?

It makes sense to do the math to figure out how much money referrals can bring in and adjust your marketing budget appropriately.

4. Identify the 'Good Fit' clients for your business.

As mentioned in earlier chapters, you should first define the ideal client before directing them to seek references.

As such, your current customers will recommend leads who genuinely make purchases from your business, as opposed to only providing names in order to receive the program's incentive.

Your client referral program should prominently feature these descriptions.

For example, if you have a form that customers must fill out, you should define a "good fit" customer immediately at the start of the form.

This will serve as a helpful reminder to attendees that you are looking for real customers, not simply friends who might be interested in your business.

5. Create a list of potential sources for referrals.

We will refer to these individuals as advocates, and they can be anyone you are now or have ever been associated to.

List them first to start. This list may include your vendors, leaders in the business, open leads, past and present clients, and so on.

You will have a strong foundation to work from thanks to this.

6. Choose the channels that will carry your show for referrals.

For your referral program to be successful, you'll need a communication platform that notifies both your company and the referred customer when a reference is made. Not only does Uber Eats know who submitted the referral when an invitation is given, but the suggested customer also receives the message.

Uber can use its marketing and sales teams to follow up with the recommended consumer once they join up using the ride credit.

Offering a $20 discount is not necessary, but your business should give clients an option to

share referrals. As such, the introduction to your organization will come from a reliable colleague rather than a cold caller.

7. Develop a plan for making contact.

Adjust now. Narrow down the list of sources and advocates to your "inner circle" of acquaintances.

These are the individuals who would recommend you without expecting anything because they see the value of your business. It is not possible to automate the process of discovering your inner circle; instead, you will benefit more from manually selecting and organizing these individuals.

There are two things to think about once you've selected your inner circle.

Above all, time is of the essence. Choose the most advantageous times to invite these inner circle champions to join your referral program. You've worked with them before, so this is a simpler process.

Examine the relationship when you start working with people who will need an incentive (as explained below).

Certain organizations may request a referral later in the relationship, depending on the service or product. After the first sale, it might be given to others.

Give it a little more time once you've inquired. This implies that it might take you several months, if not a year, to tell them about the referral scheme once more.

Additionally, you ought to choose your allies carefully, especially those closest to you.

Decide who you think is most qualified to market your brand the way it should be promoted.

Within that little circle, who do you have an amazing, fantastic relationship with? Or do you already have a happy client who found you through a recommendation?

Recall to avoid overworking your contacts and to watch out for referral fatigue.

8. Ascertain your reasons for doing things.

Referral programs fall into one of two categories: non-incentive programs or incentive programs.

At this point, you should sort your contacts into groups and determine which ones qualify for offers.

Remember the referral; ensure that they benefit from the agreement as well.

Use Uber Eats as an illustration.Customers may get $15 credits for referring friends, and they can receive $20 off their first purchase when they sign up.

9. Invest resources in informing your clientele.

After starting a referral program, make resources you think your clients would find helpful and let them know about it. Next, there should be constant promotion.

Additionally, consider various strategies to remind your clients about the program's existence in addition to the time-limited email campaign.

These include things like blogs, newsletters, email signatures with calls to action, and product updates.

You'll be aware of the resources required for each referral program once you've identified them.

Here are a few links that you may find helpful:

emails explaining your referral program to all types of contacts a description of the kinds of customers who your business works well with. You need to paint a picture of your ideal customer in their minds.

a process that directs your contacts through the application and alerts your sales team to opportunities for phone calls.

a landing page where you may get information about your contacts' buddies from them.

scripts to assist your customer care and sales representatives in describing your referral schemes.

a collection of resources, including case studies, testimonials, eBooks, videos, and anything else that offers information about working with your organization, that your contacts can forward to their friends.

Whatever media you use, be sure it aligns with the revenue, growth, and retention objectives of your program and is persistent, consistent, and not overly so.

10. Set up a mechanism for tracking.

Tracking is necessary regardless of the size of your organization (though it becomes even more important if you have a large consumer base).

This ensures that nothing is overlooked, particularly with regard to accounts that have been recommended.

It's important to record who referred them and to whom.

They were mentioned as

If they were sold or converted

How you plan to take care of them, follow up with them, and other things.

This is a great time to invest in a CRM (customer relationship management) system if you haven't already.

Customer success depends in large part on maintaining track of client relationships. Personalizing each account and relationship gives your customers the impression that they are unique members of your clientele.

11. "I'm grateful."

Express gratitude to the referrer (incentives may be useful here, but you should also think about thanking them directly) and thank the referred for joining.

Then get to work; you have happy clients to prove it.

12. As soon as you can, follow up with the people you referred.

When you do find a solid lead, don't hesitate to take advantage of it.

Keep your referrals active as soon as possible to avoid losing out on the chance to acquire these new clients.

Keep in mind that although your client might have recommended this individual to your firm, it's also possible that they recommended them to other companies.

You might also need to talk the referred customer out of a competitor they've been considering for a while because you never know what independent research the buyer has done.

Ultimately, your chances of closing the deal increase with the speed at which you can effect change.

13. Make your recommendation program more effective.

As previously said, there is no one right way to design the ideal customer referral program.

The ideal program for your company will be distinct and possibly very different from your rivals, depending on how you evaluate the needs and preferences of your clients.

The important thing to remember is that it's natural to take some time to determine what works and what doesn't. To find out what you're doing well and where you can improve, you should test your program often.

To learn what your clients think of your program, send them feedback forms. Then, make sure to use their answers going forward.

Ultimately, it is beneficial for your marketing and sales teams to receive as many leads as possible from your referral program.

After discussing the creation of a referral program, let's examine some potential implementation strategies: Customer Referral Program Ideas.

1. Freebies or competitions

Consumers may be offered freebies or contests as incentives for recommending new leads.

For instance, you may run a competition where customers may only enter if they recommend a specific amount of leads to your business. Offering an email list or getting people to sign up for a trial or subscription are a few examples of how to do this.

The only risk connected to contests is the caliber of leads. You might not receive leads interested in your business if clients pick their peers at random.

Your marketing and sales staff will have to spend time doing this as they weed out contacts who aren't a good fit for your company.

Create competitions to entice clients to recommend quality leads. If your admissions fees are determined by conversions as opposed to referrals, this is achievable.

In order to be eligible for the sweepstakes, a client must persuade others to buy your product or sign up instead of just giving their email address. This guarantees that customers who provide your business with quality leads are paid.

Why Does It Work So Well?

This strategy is effective because it plays on our innate desire to succeed. It might be a cash award or a complimentary subscription to a product or service.

Companies can reduce the size of their target market by offering clients something they desire in return for helping them locate reliable suggestions.

Who Is It Intended for?

Any firm can use this tactic as long as they have something worthwhile to give free. High-quality, high-value items can be given away for free by retailers, and service providers can offer to pay for their work for a month, six months, or a year.

How Will the Completion of the Program Be Assessed?

Ensuring that client recommendations produce high-quality referrals and conversions is a crucial aspect of success measurement. It's crucial to compare the amount of money spent on contest prizes to the total amount of money spent by customers who were referred.

When ought one to utilize it?

It makes sense to use this strategy when referral numbers start to decline. The drawback? Run it for only a predetermined period of time, like two weeks or thirty days, to maintain significant interest.

2. Charitable Giving

If your clients don't think you're trying to control them, it will be simpler to motivate them.

Offers that state, "refer five people and get 25% off," should be avoided by customers since they perceive it as an attempt to take advantage of them.

Alternatively, you can use social gifting to promote recommendations without making direct requests for them.

Rather than paying customers for a certain number of referrals, this offer incentivizes them for sharing a voucher with their peers.

Consequently, the customer receives payment each time one of their referrals redeems the certificate in addition to getting to give a gift to a buddy.

They are further inspired to connect with as many individuals as they can as a result.

Why Does It Work Well?

Social sharing gives current clients the opportunity to give and get something they will actually use. Make sure your social gift is valuable, as you are reliant on your customers to perform the legwork.

A $15 off coupon is shown in the example above for both the referrer and the referee; smaller discounts, like $5 off a purchase, are unlikely to prompt action.

Who Is It Intended for?

Businesses who have a product that qualifies for a particular or percentage discount find that social sharing is typically beneficial. This is particularly true for businesses that don't typically hold sales events because it gives clients a unique chance to buy goods at a discounted price.

How to Evaluate the Success of a Program

utilization of special coupon codes or other techniques to track the utilization of your offers one for existing customers and another for new referrals to make sure the program is profitable.

When ought one to utilize it?

Retail and e-commerce firms can use this tactic at any time of year. One piece of guidance, please? Make sure the donating is reciprocal; the transaction should benefit both the referrer and the referee.

3. Charity Auctions

Fundraisers are a great opportunity to interact with your customers' values without having to talk about your goods or services.

Engaging with a cause that matters to your customers demonstrates that you are aware of more than just their buying habits. You are aware of their expectations of your business as well as their own ideals.

Moreover, fundraisers offer a chance for referrals. Consumers may forward fundraisers to their peers with ease, and as more people engage and donate, your team will build a database of leads who align with the values of your business.

This facilitates your company's ability to follow up with these new leads and steer the conversation toward your offerings.

Why Does It Work Well?

Fundraisers draw focus to a worthy cause rather than your brand. The greatest fundraising campaigns put the cause first, even while your brand is associated with the project and might gain some goodwill as a result.

Who Is It Intended for?

Fundraising can be used as a referral scheme by any business. The concept is straightforward: plan a fundraiser for a cause dear to your customers' hearts, and then urge them to tell their friends and family about it.

How to Evaluate the Outcome of a Program.

When done well, direct referrals from fundraisers may result in the acquisition of new clients. But this is not your main objective. Instead, you want to build reputation in the community and goodwill.

Because of this, when consumers see the name of your business, they might decide to interact with it on social media or make a purchase. Find out where they heard about your business to determine how effective the fundraising campaign was.

When ought one to utilize it?

While fundraisers can be held at any time, it could be beneficial to schedule them to fall on a local holiday or festival, when patrons are more inclined to give of their time and money.

4. Customer Loyalty Tiers

Thus far, we have discussed referral program tactics that promote one-time referrals. Even though they are obviously advantageous, holding a daily competition or launching a fundraiser every other week is challenging.

Rather, a referral program that gradually leads users to recommend multiple people is more effective.

One way to achieve this is by establishing customer loyalty tiers that offer incentives to individuals who consistently suggest leads. There are incentives specific to each stage, and

Once customers have referred a particular number of leads, they are promoted to the next loyalty tier.

Using this strategy, customers are continually encouraged to refer new leads—even if you're not doing a contest or promotion.

Why Is It Beneficial?

Certain clients may be highly motivated to receive larger discounts or rewards, particularly if they make large purchases from your website or physical store.

Regardless of any incentives offered, these customers are already quite likely to stick with you and refer you to their friends and family.

Having a tier-based referral system only serves to boost incentive.

Who Is It Intended for?

Businesses that offer a broad variety of goods at different price points stand to gain from using this tactic. While higher tiers could offer both money off and first access to new products, lower tiers might just offer discounts on cheaper goods.

How to Evaluate a Program Achievement

The number of new referrals and conversions to current, high-tier clients serves as a proxy for success. If there are more high-tier members than conversions, you might want to think about adding a new tier or ending the program completely.

When ought one to utilize it?

Use this program right before launching a new product or launching a social media campaign to help boost interest in and interaction with the brand.

5. Marketing Campaigns for the Seasons

Seasonal marketing is usually a good strategy to draw in new customers.

You can provide long-term discounts that are valid throughout the year, as well as annual promotions and seasonal discounts. If you consistently carry out these initiatives, your clients will anticipate them throughout the entire year.

Why Does It Work So Well?

Major holidays are ideal for drawing clients with a compelling offer or discount because many of them see a spike in expenditure. If you execute it correctly, your clients will anticipate your seasonal marketing throughout the entire year and will spread the word to their friends.

Who Is It Intended for?

Any brand that sells goods or services can benefit from seasonal marketing as long as their messaging is consistent and they publicize the upcoming event well in advance of the season or holiday.

How to Evaluate the Success of a Program

Since these campaigns have a time limit, the number of referrals and conversions attained during the seasonal period must be compared to those of prior campaigns in order to determine the campaign's performance.

When ought one to utilize it?

Start the implementation process approximately one month before the seasonal event to give customers time to decide what they want to purchase and whom they want to recommend.

6. Special Occasions

Consumers, particularly those in small communities, enjoy having a sense of belonging.

By planning events for your customer loyalty program members, you can improve consumer advocacy and generate new leads.

For instance, you could provide extra tickets to an event so that patrons can invite their friends and introduce them to your company in a casual setting.

Rather of being taken into one of your locations, leads can attend a work outing or gathering where there is no pressure to clinch a deal.

Why Is It So Effective?

Words from the company will never carry the same weight as endorsements from friends and family.

Loyal consumers will feel at ease sending invites to their social circle if you can offer them unique experiences that showcase your brand without making it the main attraction of the whole gathering.

For whom is the intended recipient?

For B2B companies trying to improve their current corporate network connections, this is often a great approach. Establishing a reputation for organizing exceptional events can facilitate the process of current customers convincing their friends and family to attend.

Assessment of the Program's Performance

Examine the amount of money you invested in the event in relation to the number of recommendations you got and the conversions these referrals produced.

As new attendees get familiar with your events, you should expect to lose money the first few times. However, if low attendance persists, you might want to reconsider your approach.

When ought one to utilize it?

Use this technique when you have a somewhat clear calendar. For instance, the days right after the holidays are great since most potential referrals are at a low point and are looking for an excuse to party.

7. Bonuses for referrals

You can give your clients discounts based on how many leads they bring in for your business if they would prefer a more immediate reward for their recommendations.

The money you save on the price will be compensated by the leads you convert because getting new customers is considerably more expensive than keeping existing ones.

Why Does It Work So Well?

If you offer attractive products at sufficiently large discounts, you can convince clients that it's worth it for them to tell their social media contacts about your business. The drawback? Ensure that the amount of the discount is sufficient to motivate individuals to take action.

Who Is It Intended for?

This tactic works well for companies that offer expensive goods like jewelry, apparel, and gadgets. If you can provide a sizable discount in exchange for the volume of referrals you receive, your chances of success will increase.

How to Evaluate the Success of a Program

When it comes to referral programs, remember that you gain new customers for every discount you lose. Monitor sales resulting from client suggestions for a predetermined period of time say, six months to determine whether discounts are profitable.

When ought one to utilize it?

If a new, more expensive version of your product or your product line is being introduced, think about implementing this kind of marketing at that time.

8. Improvements to goods or services

Upgrades to goods or services are great incentives for customer referral programs because they draw in new business and persuade current clients to keep utilizing your offerings.

You can introduce customers to beta versions of products, services, and features that aren't available to the majority of your customer base if you don't have any fresh offerings.

Not only will your product development team's work "wow" clients, but it will also give them the impression that they are a part of an elite group with VIP access to these amazing features.

By using this tactic, you're not just giving new leads anything in return.

As you enhance the client experience over time, you're also encouraging people to provide great reviews.

Being among the "in" crowd has many benefits, particularly when it allows for early access to new features or services. Make this a memorable experience for your customers, and they will be happy to recommend your company.

Who It Works Best For: This method may work particularly well for software developers and service-oriented firms. Providing early access to new features and capabilities to loyal customers helps them feel valued and encourages them to tell others about it.

How to Evaluate the Outcome of a Program.

Getting access to these features and functionalities is extremely cost-effective because you are not already selling them to clients. Therefore, every sale brought about by recommendations is regarded as a success.

When ought one to utilize it?

Utilize a marketing of this kind each time you introduce a new good or service. Consumers are happy to be involved, and beta testing is free for you.

9. Links to Charitable Organizations

Helping your community means helping yourself.

Rather than offering discounts to customers or invitations to private events, you partner with a nearby nonprofit and donate each time a current client sends in a new lead.

Customers today prioritize integrity and reputation, which is why this is especially helpful in establishing these over time.

Why Does It Work Well?

Reputation has an impact on customer retention. While customers love a deal or a free gift, giving them something extra for every new referral improves their perception of your company and, consequently, their willingness to spread the word about your campaign.

For whom is the intended recipient?

This is a widely popular tactic. The drawback? Verify that the organization receiving your donation is one that your current clientele finds meaningful.

How to Evaluate the Success of a Program

Your goal is not quick revenue but rather reputation, so concentrate on social media shares and positive online interactions with your brand. This suggests that your promotion was effective, and conversions ought to come naturally as a result.

When ought one to utilize it?

Giving to charity is a good idea at any time of year, but it might have a bigger influence just after or during a crisis or other notable event that has people searching for ways to lend a hand.

10. Unexpected Presents

Who wouldn't value a well-considered gift?

Furthermore, although selecting a gift from a selection of options is enjoyable, being surprised is much better.

The idea behind mystery gift referrals is to deliver a surprise gift to current clients who recommend new business. It just needs to be a simple way for you to show your appreciation.

Why Does It Work So Well?

Enigmatical presents are precisely that. They deliver potential referrals a surprise, which can persuade them to follow your page, sign up for your newsletters, or start making purchases. The goal here is to be as practical as affordable.

For whom is the intended recipient?

Although any business can employ the mystery present concept, retail and e-Commerce firms who currently sell actual goods tend to find success with it.

While a software design company might give away free gifts to prospective customers, it is more challenging to connect this kind of recommendation to the service being offered.

How to Evaluate the Success of a Program

When evaluating the success of mystery presents, take expenditure into account as opposed to revenue.

If your present client base and their chances for referrals bring in enough money to pay for your gift program, keep giving them gifts. If expenses consistently outpace revenue, think about a different approach.

When ought one to utilize it?

Everyone appreciates a free gift, so whenever and wherever you can, use this tactic to bring in new business.

If you're still not sure how to put these strategies into practice, think about a few businesses that have used these customer referral ideas successfully.

Getting It to Work for You

Provide a service or product that adds value to current client accounts.

Do you have any uncertainties?Ascertain your clients' preferences prior to making a referral program investment.

1. Acorns

You will get $5 when your buddy starts making contributions to Acorns, an online micro-investment program, because you introduced them to it.

$5 may go a long way, and the concept behind Acorns is investing little amounts of money to accumulate wealth.

Sometimes, especially if they're currently utilizing a money management program, people just want money.

Getting It to Work for You

If you decide to award money for referrals, make sure the referral to deposit process is easy to comprehend and transparent.

Make sure to highlight any restrictions, such as the number of friends that customers may recommend.

2. Stitch Fix

If you recommend a friend to Stitch Fix, an online styling and purchasing service, you will receive a credit against your future order.

To find out how much you might earn, visit the Referrals tab on your account. The credit value varies.

An enticing credit or discount combined with the ease with which you may email someone a link to put on your outfit, rather than just telling them where you bought it makes this program a hit.

Getting It to Work for You

Giving up any costs associated with your services is a great place to start. The drawback? Make sure it covers everything so that they feel satisfied and that they've won.

Keep things simple, particularly if your software consists of several different parts. Think about creating a website for your referral program that goes into great detail about the procedure.

3. Healthful Paws

Healthy Paws pet insurance gives $25 to homeless pets on behalf of referrers once a referral is accomplished.

It's a smart move to provide this kind of referral for an insurance provider that specializes in animal care. Both present and potential consumers are likely to find the humanitarian tone of the award appealing.

Getting It to Work for You

Building social capital for philanthropic giving and promoting referrals are two great uses of this kind of campaign. The drawback? Be cautious while selecting charities or nonprofits to ensure their validity.

Make it obvious what charities do and how much money they raise; list them on your website and evaluate them frequently to make sure funds are being spent sensibly.

4. A food delivery service DoorDash

Doordash is always looking to hire new drivers, and its referral scheme is designed to focus on the areas where there is the greatest need.

In the event that drivers are required in their area, current drivers should check their app; if so, a "Refer Friends" banner will show up at the top of their screen.

After that, they might send email links for friends who want to work as DoorDash drivers. If these new drivers complete the necessary number of deliveries, both the referrer and the referee will be eligible for cash bonuses.

The amount earned fluctuates according on the level of demand. In places where there is a significant demand, new "Dashers" and those who recommend them can get up to $1,000. Current drivers may recommend up to 15 new drivers.

Getting It to Work for You

DoorDash is a demand-driven program. If your business offers services, this is a great way to get more people to pay attention. What is success's secret? Adapt your incentives to the needs of the community in order to promote growth where it is required.

Referees are also encouraged to work swiftly by DoorDash because they will not receive their entire bonus if their targets are not met before the change in bonuses. Although this might be a great way to spark interest, be clear about the program's operation.

A customer referral program is a great way to keep customers and boost word-of-mouth advertising. Developing brand advocates will maintain the flywheel in motion.

CHAPTER X

SUMMARY

As the landscape of digital marketing changes, businesses are continuously faced with the problem of creating fresh methods to draw in new customers. Since lead creation is the foundation of any effective marketing plan, it is an essential part of this process.

Every marketing strategy must include lead generation activities because they establish a connection between your company and its most important resource: your customers.

By identifying your target market, putting in place a solid SEO strategy, producing interesting content, making use of social media, building landing pages that convert, utilizing email and retargeting marketing, launching retargeting campaigns, and routinely reviewing and tweaking your tactics, you can greatly boost the success of your lead generation efforts.

By implementing these adjustments, your campaigns will generate more leads while also guaranteeing that these leads are of the highest caliber, increasing your conversion rates and propelling the expansion of your company.

Improved lead generation efforts from you will turn the vast internet space into a verdant field full of prospective customers simply waiting to be found.